GUIDEDGUITARARPEGGIO
PRACTICEROUTINES

Master Every Essential Guitar Arpeggio in this Comprehensive 10-Week Course

LEVICLAY

FUNDAMENTALCHANGES

Guided Guitar Arpeggio Practice Routines

Master Every Essential Guitar Arpeggio in this Comprehensive 10-Week Course

ISBN: 978-1-78933-461-6

Published by **www.fundamental-changes.com**

Copyright © 2024 Levi Clay

Edited by Tim Pettingale

Join our free Facebook Community of Cool Musicians

www.facebook.com/groups/fundamentalguitar

Instagram: **FundamentalChanges**

For over 350 Free Guitar Lessons with Videos Check Out

www.fundamental-changes.com

Cover Image Copyright: Author photo used by permission.

Contents

Introduction

It may seem strange to start an introduction by talking about what came before, but the book you're reading now is the final volume in a trilogy that builds on specific skills progressively over time, helping you to develop a deep understanding of music from an intervallic perspective.

In the first book we explored scales – the most linear form of melody – and learned that we can think of a scale simply as a set of ingredients from which we can build chords and play melodies and solos.

In the second book, we took this knowledge of intervals and applied it to chords. Chords can be thought of as harmony expressed in *vertical* form. They are a snapshot of a particular sound – collections of intervals stacked up to create different musical colours. A deep understanding of chords and how they interact with each other helps us determine which scales fit best over them.

Now, we come to the focus of this book: *arpeggios*.

So, what exactly is an arpeggio and how does it fit into this picture?

The term "arpeggio" comes from the Italian word *arpa*, meaning harp, and *arpeggiare*, meaning to play on a harp. It captures the idea of playing rich chordal sounds as individual notes. An arpeggio is a chord (vertical harmony) played in a linear manner.

The difference between arpeggios and scales lies in their relationship to the underlying harmony. When you play a scale over a certain chord, only some of the notes will belong to that chord. When you play an arpeggio, *every note* belongs to the chord, so every note is a strong melodic choice.

When students ask me, "What should I play over X chord?" I always give them the same answer: "Play X arpeggio."

Thinking in arpeggio terms takes away some of the complexity of scalic thinking. If it's an A minor chord, you can play an A minor arpeggio. If it's D7, you can play a D7 arpeggio. If it's a more complex chord like G7#9, you can play that arpeggio too. While we can also add scale tones to make our melodies more interesting, a great starting point for any solo is to just let the chords dictate what we should play.

Here we are going to explore arpeggios on the guitar in great detail. This will allow us to dig deeper into our understanding of the fretboard, but we'll also tackle the challenges of being able to play arpeggios on guitar to a high technical level. These challenges are one of the main reasons guitarists give up exploring arpeggios when they reach a certain level, but together we'll overcome them by the end of this book.

Finally, we'll bring everything full circle by examining how scales and arpeggios can work in harmony with each other (pun intended!) to help you break out of tired licks and patterns, so that you can create more dynamic, musical ideas.

How To Use This Book

As with the previous instalments in this series, the goal here is to approach the material like an old aerobics VHS tape! We're working through a set of exercises designed to focus on a key concept, then practicing it together in full.

One thing that's become clear throughout these books is that the weekly format doesn't work as well for beginners. The idea of progressing weekly is more of a long-term goal, and something you'll achieve as you develop as a player.

I've been playing guitar for over 20 years, so when I open a book like this, I'm already familiar with the concepts in each chapter and can jump right into practicing the routine. But I realise that many readers aren't at that stage yet. You may need to spend some time just learning the material before you move onto practicing each routine. And that's just fine – don't stress yourself out thinking that you're not keeping up or that everything is taking too long. Learning is a deeply personal experience, and everyone progresses at their own pace. It's perfectly fine if it takes you a little longer to master certain exercises.

You may find yourself going through this book several times, and each time it will become easier as you become more familiar with the concepts. This is the long-term goal and the reason why we practice – so that things become second nature to us. Eventually, when you're on stage, or hitting the record button in the studio, you won't have to think about what chord comes next or what arpeggio to play over it, you'll just know it.

To help the learning process go as smoothly as possible, I've recorded audio for every individual example here, as well as the full weekly routines with me talking you through the practice session. Take your time, learn the individual exercises, then move on to playing the full routine with me. When you reach the end of the book, go back to the beginning and see how much easier it feels the second time through. That's progress.

Remember, your only goal is to be better today than you were yesterday. If you keep that up, day after day, the only outcome will be reaching your goal.

Good luck!

Levi

Get the Audio

The audio files for this book are available to download for free from **www.fundamental-changes.com.** The link is in the top right-hand corner. Click on the Guitar link then simply select this book title from the drop-down menu and follow the instructions to get the audio.

We recommend that you download the files directly to your computer, not to your tablet, and extract them there before adding them to your media library. On the download page there are instructions, and we also provide technical support via the contact form.

For over 350 free guitar lessons with videos check out:

www.fundamental-changes.com

Join our free Facebook Community of Cool Musicians

www.facebook.com/groups/fundamentalguitar

Tag us for a share on Instagram: **FundamentalChanges**

Routine One: Right Hand Technique

I was playing arpeggios almost as soon as I picked up the guitar. If you hold down a C major chord and randomly pick (or fingerpick) the strings, you're literally arpeggiating the chord. Some of the first things I ever wrote were simply me picking through chords and turning them into arpeggios with my fingers.

As I hinted in the introduction, one of the biggest challenges when mastering arpeggios on the guitar is the technical skill required to play them smoothly. Think back to the work we did with chords and you'll realise that we didn't put much effort into what our picking/strumming hand was doing – it just sort of happened.

Arpeggio picking technique presents a bigger challenge. Arpeggios become more difficult to play cleanly and precisely when the playing speed increases. So, to ensure that in the future you can play anything fast that you can play slowly, I want to set you on the path of *alternate picking*.

In Example 1a we're going to arpeggiate a simple C major chord, ascending and descending. You could play this idea with sweep picking, using a series of downstrokes then upstrokes, and it would sound fine, but if the speed increased, you'd find that this method really hurt your timekeeping. So, instead we will alternate pick our way through this arpeggio. While this might feel awkward at first, you're laying a great playing foundation for future you.

I won't lie, picking one note per string using alternate picking is one of the hardest things to do on guitar. In fact, many teachers come up with systems to help their students avoid this weakness. But, here we're about facing the things we find difficult and overcoming them.

Notice the pick direction indicated above the TAB in this example. It's important to follow the symbols. The square-like symbol represents a downstroke, and the "V" symbol is an upstroke.

Example 1a:

In the next example, we'll keep the alternate picking motion but change the order of the strings we play. Although we're still using alternate picking, this change introduces a new challenge in keeping your picking consistent.

Although Example 1a could be played using a sweep picking motion, you'll see how quickly that technique falls apart when tacking Example 1b where the string order changes. Alternate picking is the way forward for good note separation and clarity.

Example 1b:

If you need further proof that alternate picking is best, let's exaggerate this idea by including more string skips in the pattern.

Example 1c:

By adding a hammer-on and altering the rhythm slightly, we can give this idea more of a bluegrass feel. Even though we're still arpeggiating a C major chord, we've introduced some rhythmic variation.

This type of picking is known as *cross-picking* in the bluegrass world and is a skill that takes time to develop. It won't improve without focused practice, but it's worth the effort.

Example 1d:

One exercise I like is to play an ascending group of three notes played four times, followed by a group of four notes on the D, G, and B strings.

As you practice, you'll notice that anchoring your hand to the bridge makes this technique harder. Instead, aim for a more free-floating hand, allowing for smoother transitions across the strings.

Start slowly, and build up speed as you go.

Example 1e:

To increase the challenge, try moving your groups of three across different sets of strings. This requires even more flexibility in your picking hand and further develops your cross-picking ability.

Example 1f:

To put this technique into a musical context, let's use it on an actual chord sequence. Here's a simple progression of G – D/F# – F – C, played with ascending arpeggios.

Example 1g:

We can make things more challenging by applying some of those three-against-four patterns to a chord movement from C major to A minor.

Example 1h:

The beauty of this technique is that once you're comfortable moving across the strings you can apply it to any chord grip. For example, try picking across an E minor with an added 9th, and a G major with an added 9th.

Example 1i:

Although alternate picking will give us the most consistent rhythmic results, we can still sweep through an open position arpeggio like that in Example 1j, and that's a valuable technique for your toolbox.

When sweeping an arpeggio like this, don't play it as a series of separate downstrokes. The motion comes from a *rest stroke*. This means, instead of picking the string in the normal way and lifting the pick away, you sound it by pushing the pick through the string so that it briefly comes to rest on the adjacent string, ready to push through to the next string. So, the sweep is a single, controlled motion that pushes through all the strings.

The best way to develop this technique is by strumming the chord normally then gradually slowing down the motion until you produce a more distinct, arpeggiated chord. We'll do this in the following example, and once the motion feels natural, focus on repeating the pattern with as much rhythmic consistency as possible.

Example 1j:

We can take this idea and apply it to just the middle of an arpeggio to create a pattern similar to *The House of the Rising Sun* by The Animals. Here, I've applied it to A minor and C major chords.

Example 1k:

To finish up this routine, I've included some longer examples that will help you work on both rhythmic evenness and left-hand stamina.

The first example is something I covered in my *Hybrid Picking Guitar Technique* book, which is Bach's Prelude in C. I suggest alternate picking this for rhythmic accuracy but feel free to experiment with rest stroke sweeping (notated in bars 1-2) as well.

Example 1l:

Next is an eight-bar idea that follows a chord progression with more of a bluegrass picking pattern, combining single-note arpeggios with chord strums. Remember, your fretting hand is simply holding down a chord while the picking hand creates melodic interest by arpeggiating.

Example 1m:

Another useful warm-up for the picking hand that creates some beautiful sounds is to take a basic CAGED E shape barre chord and, leaving the top two strings open, move it around the fretboard. I remember hearing guitarists like Alex Lifeson and John Petrucci do this and loving the effect. Let the open strings ring out and you'll get some lovely harmonies.

Example 1n:

That's it for the first routine. There's plenty to get your teeth into here and it's a good introduction to the techniques you'll need for upcoming chapters. You really can't spend too much time on these techniques. Everything you invest here will lead to greater confidence on the guitar and the ability to play ideas that many players avoid.

Take your time with these picking exercises, and try applying them to your own chord progressions to gradually build proficiency.

Get to work, and I'll see you next week!

Routine: Two Vertical Triads

We've spent some time getting the basic picking technique in place and applying it to chords. Throughout the rest of the book, keep applying that alternate picking approach and you'll be well on the way to mastering it thoroughly. Now we've put that foundation in place, it's time to start thinking about how we organise arpeggios on the fretboard.

As with scales and chords, the key to gaining a deep, practical understanding of arpeggios lies in applying a system of organisation to the theory. If you understand how arpeggios are constructed and have a good method for organising them on the fretboard, you'll be pretty unstoppable.

We'll start by reviewing triads and applying them in three basic positions. These arpeggios will move across the strings rather than along them, so I think of these as *vertical* configurations. Just as we visualise scales around chord forms, we want to do the same with our arpeggios.

Let's begin with major triads, which consist of a root (1), a 3rd (3), and a 5th (5). For example, if we take an E shape C major chord in its barre form, as in Example 2a, and examine its intervals, we have:

R 5 R 3 5 R.

This is almost a complete triad arpeggio and all we need to do is add the missing 3rd between the first root and the 5th to get all the triad notes in order.

When we reach the top of the arpeggio we land back on the root note. When playing this type of major triad shape, if the root is at the 8th fret, then the 3rd will be four frets higher at the 12th fret.

Our first exercise uses this pattern to create a looping arpeggio. While playing it, actually speak the names of the intervals out loud to reinforce your understanding.

Example 2a:

One of the best ways to start integrating arpeggios into your playing is by breaking them into smaller fragments. One approach is to use sequences where the arpeggio is played in groups of four notes. These sequences are challenging for both your picking and fretting hands, so take your time to ensure each note is cleanly separated. We're playing melodies, not strumming chords.

Example 2b:

Another great way to practice this concept is to re-finger the arpeggio so that it includes all the closed-voiced triads I covered in *Guided Guitar Chord Practice Routines*. In this example, we will add some rhythm to break the arpeggio into three-note groupings, making it easier to distinguish from the full six-string pattern.

Example 2c:

We can apply the same idea to different chord positions. For instance, if we move down the neck to the A shape, we can play another C major triad arpeggio that fits around this chord form.

Example 2d:

The stretch from the 3rd to the 8th fret can be difficult if you have smaller hands and part of playing guitar is recognising your physical limitations and what you can and can't pull off. If the A shape C major triad feels too much, try shifting up to a G major arpeggio, which you'll find a lot easier. As always, these stretches will become easier with practice.

For an extra challenge, play the A shape arpeggio and, when you reach the top, shift up and descend using the E shape arpeggio.

Example 2e:

```
C
     ---------------------------------3----8---12----8------------------------
     ----------------------5----5-----------------------8---------------------
     ---------------2---5-----------------------------------9-----------------
     ----------2---------------------------------------------10---10---7------
     ----3------------------------------------------------------------8----3--
     ------------------------------------------------------------------------
```

The C shape arpeggio is probably the most comfortable as it doesn't require any awkward rolling motions with the fretting hand.

Example 2f:

```
C
     --13-------------------------------12---15---12-----------------------------
     --12----------------------13--13----------------13---12---------------------
     --14------------14---12--------------------------------14-------------------
     --15---15----------------------------------------------------15---15--------
     -------------------------------------------------------------------15-------
     ---------------------------------------------------------------------------
```

Let's now ascend through the E shape, shift into the C shape, and descend.

Example 2g:

```
C
     -----------------------------8---12---15---12-------------------------------
     ---------------------8---8---------------13---------------------------------
     ------------9---------------------------------12---------------------------
     -----10---10-------------------------------------14------------------------
     --7------------------------------------------------15---15---12------------
     --8------------------------------------------------------------------------
```

Position shifting through arpeggios across multiple octaves can be tough on your hands and isn't necessarily how we'd play arpeggios in a real-world setting, but they provide a great technical workout.

Remember that when we're practicing, we're exercising our minds not just our hands, so let's practice arpeggios through the Circle of Fifths to keep mentally engaged. To start, we'll just play them ascending with a held note at the end, so we can mentally prepare for the next chord.

The Circle of Fifths pattern is:

C F Bb Eb Ab Db Gb B E A D G

You may notice that when I play an A shape arpeggio, sometimes I'll play the 3rd on the A string and other times on the D string.

Example 2h:

E   A

```
T
A
B
                    12
                 12       12              12
              13        13                    14   12—17
           14        14                  14        14
        11—14     11—14              11—14      11—14
     12        12                 12         12
```

D   G

```
T
A
B
                 10          10           10—15        10—15
              10        10        12           12
           11        11        12          12
        12        12       10—14       10—14
     9—12      9—12
  10        10
```

To really develop your ability to think and visualise faster on the fretboard, you need to put your brain under a bit of stress during practice. We'll do that here by adding the descending version of the arpeggio as you think about which key comes next.

Example 2i:

C   F

```
T
A
B
                    8—12—8       8
                 8           8
              9           9
           10         10—7
        7—10              8
     8
```

B♭   E♭

```
T
A
B
                 10—13—10
              11        11
           10        10
        12        12
     13        13—13
              13
```

If you want to take this idea to the next level, you need to practice changing from one arpeggio to the next on any string. A good way to do this is to slow down the pulse to 1/4 notes and focus on connecting to the nearest note in the next arpeggio when the chord changes.

Example 2j:

Now let's change things up by converting these major triad arpeggios into minor triads. Instead of thinking of these as "new" shapes, think of them as the major shapes you already know, but you're lowering the 3rds (E) to flat 3rds (Eb). Here's an example using the E shape, with a triplet rhythm for some variety.

Example 2k:

Here's the same idea, now moved up to the C shape.

Example 2l:

And finally, here it is in the A shape.

Example 2m:

These exercises will help get your fretting hand in sync with solid alternate picking. Once you're comfortable with these shapes, a good challenge is to link them up by ascending one position and descending the next. Here's an example with a C minor chord.

Example 2n:

Major and minor triads are essential to know, but there are also three other types of triad you need to know: diminished (1 b3 b5), augmented (1 3 #5), and suspended (1 2 5 and 1 4 5).

Here are the three C diminished triad arpeggios. To play these, I visualise a C minor arpeggio and lower the 5ths (G) to b5s (Gb). These shapes don't come up too often, but they're great for interval practice.

Example 2o:

Next, here are the three C augmented triads. To play these, I visualise C major and raise all the 5ths (G) to #5s (G#) You'll notice that these shapes are essentially identical as the augmented triad is symmetrical – each note is the same distance (two tones) apart.

Example 2p:

Now, let's look at the three Csus2 arpeggios. These are great for adding a more ambiguous sound to your solos.

Example 2q:

Finally, here are the three Csus4 arpeggios.

Example 2r:

It's important to acknowledge that a lot more work can be done on the ideas we've covered here. For example, once you feel comfortable, you could incorporate sequences of fours, take the arpeggios through the Circle of Fifths, or link positions into one long example.

The first step is making sure you know all these arpeggios in their most common forms and can play them automatically. Once that becomes second nature, you'll have more mental energy to focus on applying them in different musical contexts.

Routine Three: Horizontal Triads

True mastery of the fretboard comes when you start breaking free of the limitations of the box patterns you learned as a beginner. In the last chapter, we worked with triad arpeggios using the E, A, and C shapes, and briefly touched on the horizontal approach by shifting between positions as we moved up the fretboard. Horizontal movement along the string is an important skill, and it's something we want to be able to do seamlessly at any time on any string.

We can develop this skill in a methodical way by playing intervals and varying the number of notes we play on each string. A simple pattern-based approach is to take a C major triad and organize it in a 1-2-1-2-1-2 pattern across the strings, so that we play one note on the first string, two on the next, one on the following, and so on.

To finger this, use the middle, index and pinkie finger, then shift up to play the note on the D string with the middle finger, then repeat.

Example 3a:

We can also arrange this triad in a 2-1-2-1-2-1 pattern.

Example 3b:

Let's turn the C major triad into a C minor triad by flattening all the E notes to Eb. Now practice ascending and descending through both finger patterns with this new minor triad.

Example 3c:

If we pause to consider the intervals and the relationships between them, it opens up new possibilities for fingering these triads.

In a major triad, we have a root, 3rd, 5th, then we add the root an octave higher. The interval between the root and 3rd is a major third (four frets); the interval between the 3rd and 5th is a minor third (three frets); and the distance from the 5th to the higher root is a perfect fourth (five frets).

When we play a triad, we can think of it as the movement, "up a major 3rd, up a minor 3rd, up a perfect 4th" and repeat. If we play this for G major on a single string, it looks like this, played first on the E string, then on the D string, then on the B string.

Example 3d:

It's not practical from a musical point of view to play triads as four-note-per-string patterns, but the previous exercise helped us to learn the intervals. Once we can clearly "hear" those intervals, and know which note to go to next, we can finger triads in many different ways.

I've written out three possible fingerings for G major in Example 3e. As you play through them, pay attention to both the sound of the intervals and where they're located.

Example 3e:

To become more fluent on the fretboard, let's focus on transitioning at different points on each string. In this next exercise, we'll move from the E shape to the C shape, first transitioning on the E string, then the A string, then the D string, and so on.

We'll do this in both ascending and descending patterns.

Example 3f:

Now do the same exercise moving from the C shape up to the A shape.

Example 3g:

And finally, let's practice moving from the A shape to the E shape.

Example 3h:

Instead of writing these exercises out again for minor triads, I want you to apply the same concepts as earlier to the following triads and work them into your practice routine.

The distances between the intervals in a minor triad are slightly different. From the root (1) to the b3 is a minor 3rd. From the b3rd the 5th is a major 3rd. From the 5th back up to the root the distance is a 4th. We'll start with a G minor arpeggio in the E shape, and make transitions on the D, G, and high E strings.

Example 3i:

It's worth noting that the more you work on ideas like this, the more you'll discover which patterns feel natural to play, and which ones you can safely discard. I favour transitions that feel comfortable to my hand because those are the ones I'll be able to play effortlessly in the midst of a solo.

If we move to a C minor triad in the A shape, we can begin low on the neck and transition up into the higher position. This approach mirrors the octave patterns we discussed earlier in the chapter, where we played a three-note idea and shifted it up in octave patterns across two strings.

Example 3j:

But we don't have to stick to those patterns, and we can create something with even more range, as in the following example. Notice how I ascend and descend slightly differently. This variation helps to keep me on my toes.

Example 3k:

If we switch to a D minor triad, we can start in the C shape and move all the way up the neck to the E shape which gives us another useful position shift.

Example 3l:

For an even wider range, we can use an E minor triad. With the open E string available, we can extend the arpeggio even further. If you have a guitar with 24 frets there's nothing stopping you from taking this arpeggio up to the highest notes, creating a full four-octave spread.

Example 3m:

To wrap up this routine, I want to push you a bit further by applying a melodic sequence to these horizontal patterns and combining both major and minor triads.

In the following example, we'll use a C major to A minor progression and play an ascending sequence of fours.

Example 3n:

If we transpose this progression to the key of G, we have a G major to E minor sequence which gives us a completely different pathway up and down the neck.

Example 3o:

We haven't discussed picking in this chapter, but these ideas have to be alternate picked. With so many position changes, they go against the different systems guitar players use to sweep pick. But, the great benefit of these exercises is that they will increase your fretboard knowledge and give you a greater level of melodic control.

The more you can break out of traditional box patterns, the more freedom you'll have when playing melodically using both arpeggios and scales.

There's no shortcut with this stuff! You just need to improve your brain's ability to visualise these pathways and train your hands to keep up with where they need to be.

Routine Four: Triad Progression Workouts

We've looked at a little bit of technique and worked through a series of fingering options for triad arpeggios, but one of the best ways to get to grips with arpeggios is to apply them in a musical way. So, in this chapter we'll play some longer etudes that outline different chord positions in various ways. Sometimes we'll stay within a single position, while other times we'll challenge ourselves to break out of the usual box patterns and cover more of the neck.

Let's start with the classic arpeggios found at the end of *Sultans of Swing*. The chord progression is:

Dm – Bb – C – C

There are countless ways to arpeggiate this progression, but a good starting point is to use two-string arpeggios, which is how Mark Knopfler plays them.

Example 4a:

From here, let's expand the chord progression into a three-string looping arpeggio pattern that stays in the same position.

Example 4b:

For a more challenging approach, we can jump between different positions and inversions, still using three-string patterns but adding some complexity. I've ended this example with a big descending D minor arpeggio.

Example 4c:

Example 4d is a much trickier etude as we play the chord changes twice as quickly and cover all six strings in the process.

34

Example 4d:

It's common in rock and metal tunes to have a section with a set chord progression, which the guitarist will outline with an arpeggio pattern. You could stick with familiar patterns used by players like Yngwie Malmsteen or Jason Becker, but there's no reason why you can't write your own arpeggio lines that incorporate more intricate points of transition.

Example 4e:

While classic rock offers great progressions for arpeggios, looking to the world of classical music is a great way to find progressions to work on. One of the most well-known examples is Johann Pachelbel's *Canon in D*, a piece so famous that it arguably makes Pachelbel the original one-hit wonder!

Canon in D follows a repeating chord sequence of D – A – Bm – F#m – G – D – G – A.

This progression is perfect for warming up with full six-string arpeggios, either starting from the top or bottom of each arpeggio.

Example 4f:

But there are countless ways to approach arpeggios and here's another variation you can explore.

Example 4g:

We can raise the difficulty level by channelling some Jason Becker influence and play triplets with sweep picking to create a more technical feel.

After all the alternate picking you've been doing, take your time with this one. Learn it slowly and make sure you control the picking hand well to keep the sweeps smooth and consistent.

Example 4h:

As with any arpeggio idea, the real challenge is to break out of predictable patterns and become comfortable with changing chords on any string. Here's a more melodically engaging etude that shifts between chords in less expected ways.

Example 4i:

Here's another etude based on the Canon played higher up the neck with more challenging transitions. I love working on etudes like this. Though I've only included two here, I could easily fill a book with these kinds of studies.

Once you're comfortable with the examples I've provided, try composing some of your own. Since we're only using notes from the triads, the limited note pool should mean you can come up with something fresh if you take your time.

Example 4j:

For our final progression we'll stay in the classical world, this time drawing inspiration from Beethoven's famous *Moonlight Sonata*. I've simplified it by treating the dominant chords as major triads, but it's still a wonderful way to practice arpeggios.

Unlike the previous progression, we're now in a minor key (C# Minor) and in 12/8 time, so each bar contains four triplet groupings. To start, we'll play simple ascending and descending arpeggios.

Example 4k:

Now, let's embrace the triplet feel of the piece by playing three-note groupings of closed-voiced triads that outline the chord changes.

Example 4l:

Even though the piece has a triplet feel, we don't have to limit ourselves to three-note groupings. In fact, it can be interesting to play groups of four, creating a rhythmic feel of four-against-three.

Example 4m:

To really stretch our arpeggio muscles, it's fun to play etudes that cover the entire neck while twisting and turning through unexpected positions. These studies require deep fretboard control, and while you can learn etudes like this by heart, your long-term goal is to develop enough fretboard freedom to improvise through chord changes seamlessly. That might seem intimidating, but the concept is simple: when a chord happens, just play the notes in that chord!

Example 4n:

Finally, I wanted to come up with something even more challenging for you. Instead of sticking to stepwise motion with our arpeggios, we'll break them into wider spread, open-voiced triads. These are much harder to navigate because we have to skip strings between each note.

You'll find it difficult to memorise this etude if you haven't spent enough time learning your chord voicings, but these are all open-voiced grips we covered in my guided chord practice book. If you struggle with this, it might be a sign that you need to revisit some of that foundational work. Don't hesitate to go back and reinforce those basics!

Example 4o:

That's plenty of triad work for now. There's much more to arpeggios than just three-note chords, but I wanted you to master these before moving on to the richer, more complex chords in the following chapters.

Routine Five: Diatonic 7th Arpeggios

With our triad workout complete, it's time to get a little jazzier by adding an additional note to turn our triads into 7th chords.

In this routine, we'll build on the triad knowledge we've developed, exploring all the 7th arpeggios we're likely to need, using both vertical and horizontal fingering systems.

Let's start by brushing up on the theory behind 7th chords.

In the key of C, a C major triad consists of the intervals 1 (root), 3 (major 3rd), and 5 (perfect 5th). These notes are chosen by selecting every other note from the major scale (C D E F G A B). I.e., we take the first note (C), skip the second, take the 3rd note (E), skip the 4th, and take the 5th note (G).

If we continue this pattern and add a fourth note, we get the intervals:

1 3 5 7

This forms a Cmaj7 chord.

Major 7 chords are a major triad with an added 7th from the major scale. It's useful to know that the 7th is always located a semitone below the root note.

As we work through this chapter, we'll look at how each type of 7th arpeggio is constructed, but first let's work with the major 7th.

Major 7 Arpeggios

Let's play a Cmaj7 arpeggio based around our triad E shape. Note that there are two options for where we play the 7th interval at the top of the arpeggio: either on the high E string or the B string.

Example 5a:

As you work through the arpeggios in this chapter, focus on where the new note (7th) is located and memorise its position relative to the rest of the arpeggio. Get familiar with the placement of this interval, so that you never forget where it is.

Here are two options for playing a Cmaj7 arpeggio around the A shape.

Example 5b:

Cmaj7

```
T|-5-----------------3--7----8-7-3----------------------------------4-----5-|
A|-4--------------4-5-----------------5-4----------------------2--5----------|
 |-5--------2--5--------------------------5-2-----------------------------------|
B|-3--3--------------------------------------3-2------2-3------------------|
                                                     3                    |
```

```
T|-----------------3--7----8-7-3--------------------------------4-----5--:|
A|-------------4-5-----------------5-4----------------------------------------|
 |-----5-------------------------------5-----------------5----------------:|
B|-3--7------------------------------------7----3------3--7---------------|
                                           7--3--7                        |
```

For the C shape chord there's only really one practical way to play the Cmaj7 arpeggio.

Example 5c:

Cmaj7

```
T|-12-----------------12-15-12--------13-12------------------------------12----15--:|
A|-12-------------12-13------------------------12------------------12-13----------|
 |-14--------14--------------------------------14------------------14------------|
B|-15--15------------------------------15-14----------14-15---------------------|
                                        15-12---15-----------------------------|
```

One of the beautiful things about 7th arpeggios is that they lend themselves really well to creating small, two-string motifs that can be moved up and down the neck in octaves. It's a great way to incorporate horizontal movement and position shifts.

Example 5d:

There are lots of two-string patterns that work well when moving in octaves and finding these can quickly help to expand your fretboard knowledge.

Example 5e:

The best way to really get to grips with arpeggios on the fretboard is to come up with some of your own long, flowing etudes that cover the entire neck. As in previous chapters, the aim of such exercises is to work on seeing/hearing the distance from one arpeggio tone to the next. Once you can do this on adjacent strings and with position shifts, you'll be able to do anything!

Here's an example of a flowing Cmaj7 arpeggio etude.

Example 5f:

Here's a similar idea that begins higher up the neck and descends.

Example 5g:

Dominant 7 Arpeggios

If we take a Cmaj7 arpeggio and lower the 7th by a semitone we create the intervals 1 3 5 b7, which is the formula for a C dominant 7 (C7) arpeggio and gives us the notes C E G Bb.

It's useful to know that the b7 is a tone below the root.

Example 5h:

If we apply that formula to our A, E, and C shapes, we create the following arpeggios. When learning these shapes, view them as the major triads you already know, but with an added b7.

Example 5i:

You could also play these arpeggios in each of the five CAGED forms.

Example 5j:

This is the part where things get interesting, because when I use dominant 7 arpeggios to solo over dominant 7 chords, I almost always add a chromatic note to the shape. Chromatic notes are very useful in an arpeggio context, just to add a bit of movement and interest.

A typical thing I do is to add the b3 as a chromatic approach note to the 3rd. This b3 often occurs on a weak part of the bar (an off-beat) and resolves to the 3rd on a stronger beat.

This begs the question: is it still an arpeggio?

Technically, we're adding notes that aren't in the chord, but the idea of using the notes of the arpeggio to outline the chord remains. For me, this chromatic note just helps to make this arpeggio sound more musical.

It's worth noting that this movement always occurs as an ascending idea (i.e., b3 ascending to the 3rd, and never 3rd descending to b3), even when the actual melody descends the arpeggio.

So we would play,

1 b7 5 *b3-3* 1

Not,

1 b7 5 *3-b3* 1.

You can see this in the idea below.

Example 5k:

We can actually add several notes and still think of it as an arpeggio, as long as targeting arpeggio notes is the core concept.

The next example begins with a chromatic connection from the 3rd up to 5th, followed by a b3 to 3rd motion, and ends with a phrase that goes 4th, b3, 3rd. While this isn't a pure arpeggio, it's certainly an arpeggio-based idea and definitely not a scale line!

After playing this in the C shape, move it down an octave and play it around the E shape.

Example 5l:

This may all seem like a bit of a detour, but it's been a valuable exercise because it's helped to reinforce the location of the b3 interval, which brings us onto the minor 7 (m7) arpeggio.

Minor 7 arpeggios

If we take a dominant 7 arpeggio (1 3 5 b7) and lower the 3rd, we create the intervals 1 b3 5 b7.

This forms a minor triad with a b7, which is a minor 7 chord. In the key of C that gives us the notes C Eb G Bb.

Here's how that looks around the E shape.

Example 5m:

Once you know the intervals that make up the arpeggio, you can easily apply them to our three basic A, E, and C chord forms.

Example 5n:

A great exercise to reinforce your knowledge of an arpeggio is to apply a pattern of ascending and descending "fours", where we ascend four notes of the arpeggio, jump back down to the second note we played, and repeat this pattern as we gradually ascend.

This exercise is not just musical, it quickly helps you to identify any technical issues you have with fingering the arpeggios in each position.

Here's the ascending and descending fours pattern around the E shape. Once you've mastered it here, apply it to the other three positions of every arpeggio type in this chapter.

Example 5o:

Another fantastic way to break up a position is by playing a note-skipping idea. Play the first note of the arpeggio, skip the second, and jump to the third note. Now return to the note you skipped and repeat the process.

Again, ideas like this will immediately bring up technical issues for you to overcome. Apply this pattern to every arpeggio voicing in this chapter.

Example 5p:

m7b5 arpeggios

The final arpeggio we'll cover is the minor 7b5. This could be considered the ugly stepsister of our diatonic arpeggios, but while it may feel awkward at first, it has many great uses.

To create it we take a minor 7 arpeggio (1 b3 5 b7) and lower the 5th to build an arpeggio that has the intervals 1 b3 b5 b7.

This arpeggio exists naturally in the major scale and is formed when we harmonise the 7th degree.

Here's it is played around the E shape.

Example 5q:

Now let's play it around the A, E, and C shapes.

Example 5r:

It may feel like we've rushed through these arpeggio types, but we're just laying foundations here. We'll be getting into them in much more detail over the coming weeks as we look at how to apply them.

For now, practice these arpeggio patterns in different keys. Once you're comfortable, try the sequencing ideas you learned above and try to create your own pathways from the bottom to the top of the neck.

Don't rush the process, as familiarity with these patterns will allow you to apply them musically to chord progressions when soloing. Put in the time, and you'll see the results!

Routine Six: 7th Chord Progression Workouts

There's no better way to work on your arpeggio skills than by applying them to real music. I grew up listening to heavy metal and later got into country, and the truth is, there aren't that many 7th chords found in those genres. So, to practice your fluency, you might need to step outside your usual listening habits.

Jazz is the perfect place to go for this. Now, I know what you're thinking, "Jazz?! Eww!" But don't worry, I'm not talking about smoky clubs and abstract jazz, where the only people listening are other musicians with their arms folded. I mean the *old* jazz standards, often referred to as the Great American Songbook.

These were the popular songs of their day, often sung by iconic artists like Nat King Cole, Bing Crosby, Tony Bennett, Dean Martin, or Chet Baker. Songs like *Fly Me to the Moon*, *The Way You Look Tonight* and *Summertime* are still loved today because they have beautiful melodies and interesting harmonies.

The main way I work on my arpeggios today is by opening an app like iReal Pro and picking one of the thousands of jazz standard chord charts. Then, I will arpeggiate my way through it. The best approach is to listen to the song you're going to work on first, so that your ear can connect with the harmony and you have an idea of the sound you're aiming for, then work through it.

In my guided chord routine book, I used the progression to *All of Me* as a reference. Let's start with that tune, since you might already be familiar with it. However, you can (and should) take all these exercises and apply them to as many songs as possible.

Start by arpeggiating each chord, beginning from the root note on the E or A string.

Example 6a:

Once you feel you're getting to grips with this, move on to ascending one arpeggio and descending the next. I'm sticking to 1/4 notes here to keep things simple and not overload our brains.

Example 6b:

In the previous example, we changed arpeggio at the top or bottom of each pattern, which is easier to do, but sticking to that approach won't give us the freedom we're looking for – we need to challenge ourselves. So, now we'll move to 1/8th notes and change arpeggios mid-pattern, on whatever string we happen to be playing when the chord changes.

Example 6c:

E7 **Am7**

D7 **Dm7** **G7**

Another way to push yourself is by adding a limitation. For example, playing the arpeggios on only the top three strings will force you to visualise the fretboard differently.

Example 6d:

Cmaj7 **E7** **A7** **Dm7**

E7 **Am7** **D7** **Dm7** **G7**

Now let's switch to the Jerome Kern standard *All the Things You Are*. I like this one because the chord changes happen more frequently (almost every bar), and it covers all four basic chord qualities.

As before, the first step should be listening to some recordings of the song to get familiar with how it sounds. Then, review the chord symbols to understand the harmony. Just like *All of Me*, we'll start by arpeggiating each chord in an ascending pattern.

Example 6e:

That's a lot of chords to remember! The task can be made much easier if we break the progression down into manageable eight-bar chunks and look for patterns that we recognise, so there's less to think about while we're playing.

Think back to the Circle of Fifths pattern we discussed and you'll spot some clear patterns here.

Starting on F and moving around the circle, we get:

F Bb Eb Ab Db

These are the first five chords of the progression!

Then there is a Dm7 chord. Moving from there we have D G C – another three consecutive notes on the Circle of Fifths.

When looking at chord charts like this, dominant chords can help us to identify the key, since each key has only one dominant chord. The Eb7 in bar three tells us we're in Ab Major. So, the first five chords form the sequence:

vi – ii – V – I – IV

Or,

Fm7 – Bbm7 – Eb7 – AbMaj7 – DbMaj7

Then, we modulate to C Major and play:

ii – V – I

Or,

Dm7 – G7 – Cmaj7

Let's play through this eight-bar chunk in 1/8th notes.

Example 6f:

We should aim to be able to play this anywhere on the neck.

Example 6g:

The next eight bars of the tune are actually just a repeat of the previous eight bars but played a 4th higher. Without looking at the chords, we can simply follow the Circle of Fifths:

Cm7 – Fm7 – Bb7 – EbMaj7 – AbMaj7

Then, we move up a semitone and play another ii – V – I, this time in G Major:

Am7 – D7 – Gmaj7

Example 6h:

Here's another run through those arpeggios, this time higher up the neck.

Example 6i:

The next eight bars contain two ii – V – I progressions, one in G and one in E:

Am7 – D7 – Gmaj7

Then,

F#m7b5 – B7 – Emaj7

Notice that the second ii – V – I starts with a m7b5 ii chord, but resolves to a *major* rather than a minor chord, which creates an unexpected but pleasant variation in the song.

The section ends with a C7, which sets up the Fm7 in the next bar.

Example 6j:

Being able to arpeggiate through ii – V – I progressions like this is incredibly beneficial. It will do wonders for both your fretboard knowledge and your ear as you internalise what it sounds like to navigate functional harmony.

Example 6k:

The final section mirrors the first, but with a little diversion when we arrive at Dbmaj7. From there, the chord quality shifts to a minor 7, followed by a chromatic descent to Bbm7 (the ii of the key) and resolves home to the I chord via the V chord, another ii – V – I sequence. So, that is:

Fm7 – Bbm7 – Eb7 – AbMaj7 – DbMaj7 – Dbm7 – Cm7 – Bdim7 – Bbm7 – Eb7 – AbMaj7

Let's arpeggiate through that.

Example 6l:

So far, we've played everything as long runs of 1/8th notes. While that is a great challenge for the mind, it's not the most rewarding exercise for the ear, so let's take the final ii – V – I and add some rhythmic variety to make it more musical.

Simple syncopation can transform these arpeggios into something much more expressive.

Example 6m:

Here's another example in a higher position on the neck.

Example 6n:

To finish up this routine, I'll improvise through the entire progression, playing only notes from the arpeggios and breaking them up with rhythmic variations.

Example 60:

Of course, we're still only scratching the surface of what's possible. We haven't even started adding in notes outside of the arpeggios! While it might be tempting to rush ahead, spending time mastering the basic four-note arpeggios, and figuring out as many ways as possible to lay them out on the neck, will feel like a superpower when we begin incorporating more advanced ideas later.

I've said it before and I'll say it again, we're building on solid foundations here, not quicksand, so, get to work!

Routine Seven: Chord Scale Arpeggios

Until now, we've only played arpeggios that match the chord we're playing. For example, if the chord is Cmaj7, we've played a Cmaj7 arpeggio. But this isn't the only way to approach arpeggios. In fact, we can play other arpeggios that are built from the notes of the parent scale that the chord belongs to.

This approach requires both a strong knowledge of the chords that belong to a key and solid fretboard visualisation.

First, we're going to learn how to move between all the arpeggios and triads that can be built on each note of a scale as the chords change, but later we'll learn how we can play these ideas over different chords to create rich solos that contain *extensions* on the original chord.

Let's start by refreshing our memory of the diatonic chords in a key. In the key of C Major, the chords are:

Cmaj7 – Dm7 – Em7 – Fmaj7 – G7 – Am7 – Bm7b5

The pattern of chord *qualities* (major 7 and minor 7 etc) is consistent in any major key:

- Chords 1 and 4 are always major 7

- Chord 5 is always dominant 7

- Chords 2, 3, and 6 are always minor 7

- Chord 7 is always minor 7b5

Let's play these diatonic arpeggios consecutively in the A shape.

Example 7a:

Bm7♭5

Cmaj7

If we move to the key of G Major, we can apply the same formula to the notes in the G Major scale:

Gmaj7 – Am7 – Bm7 – Cmaj7 – D7 – Em7 – F#m7b5

Let's play these arpeggios in the E shape.

Example 7b:

Gmaj7 **Am7** **Bm7**

Cmaj7 **D7** **Em7**

F♯m7♭5 **Gmaj7**

Now, let's jump back to the key of C and stay in the E shape. This time we'll ascend through each of the diatonic arpeggios but stay in position. This exercise will teach you to build arpeggios from any finger on any string.

When I do this, I like to say the name of the arpeggio I'm moving to. Try it – it connects the name of the arpeggio with its fingering pattern, making the process more about visualisation than memorising a long string of notes.

Example 7c:

In the previous example, I made things easier by allowing you two beats of rest between each chord change. Let's now remove those rests and connect all the arpeggios as one continuous stream of 1/8th notes so it sounds a bit more fluent.

Example 7d:

Another approach is to ascend one arpeggio and descend the next. Try this descending from the top strings too.

Example 7e:

This is something you should be able to do in any position on the neck. Let's play our ascending arpeggios in the A shape.

Example 7f:

Or try playing them around the C shape. Again, figure out how to begin from different strings and ascend or descend from wherever you start. This can form hours of musical practice.

Example 7g:

We don't have to limit ourselves to 7th arpeggios as triads work just as well! If we go back to the E shape and play a mix of ascending and descending triads, it looks like this. Notice how the rhythm of two 1/8th notes followed by a 1/4 note places each triad into its own two-beat phrase.

Example 7h:

Dm   Em   F   Em   Dm   C   Bdim   Am

G   F   Em   Dm   C   Bm   C

If we play this series as straight 1/8th notes, we create an interesting three-against-four feel.

Example 7i:

So, here's an interesting question… Are we playing arpeggios, triads, or scales? Well, we're playing triad arpeggios but we're also playing all seven notes of the major scale.

Remember that the goal of this book is ultimately to blur the lines between chords, scales and arpeggios, allowing for complete freedom in your playing. So, while I'm thinking of all these examples as arpeggiated ideas, since I'm focusing on triads, they could easily be viewed as scale patterns too. Neither is wrong.

We can push this concept even further by adding a chromatic approach note leading into each triad. In the next example, the chromatic approach notes are shown in brackets.

Example 7j:

When descending, we still add a chromatic approach below the first note of each triad. You can also slide when you need to shift position with the index finger. For example, when targeting the 7th fret on the D string, you can slide up from the 6th fret with the index finger.

Example 7k:

Here's an example of ascending and descending triads around the A shape with added chromatic approach notes.

Example 7l:

Now, let's add chromatic approach notes to 7th arpeggios. A common method is to place the chromatic note right before the beat, sliding up into the arpeggio, then ascending with a triplet feel. Here's how that sounds with the diatonic chords of C Major.

Example 7m:

Staying in one position is more challenging than shifting up and down the neck. Neither approach is better, they're just different ways to navigate the fretboard. However, to become a more fluent player you'll need the freedom to do both.

Here's an example of diatonic arpeggios in C Major ascending the neck without any chromaticism.

Example 7n:

Now, let's add chromatic tones to connect these positions. Even if you don't consider yourself a chromatic player, practicing these ideas will help you move around the fretboard with more fluidity and less fear.

Example 7o:

As with everything in this book, we're only scratching the surface of what's possible with arpeggios. There are countless ways to outline chords, and you don't have to stick to only the notes of the chord you're playing. We'll explore this more later.

Spend some time with these concepts then we'll dive deeper in the next routine where we'll explore how to combine arpeggios and scales in a more fluid way.

Routine Eight: Combining Arpeggios & Scales

Now we're getting into the really interesting stuff. You might be wondering, "If this is a book on arpeggios, why are we talking about scales?"

Well, one of the worst things you can do in your musical development is to think of arpeggios, triads and scales as separate "boxes", when the reality is that beautiful music blurs the lines between them so seamlessly that it's hard to say where one ends and the other begins.

I spent many years working on scales and arpeggios separately, and when it came to playing, everything sounded formulaic and predictable. I was just cycling through things I'd learned with no real freedom, and it became a bit of a prison for me.

It just wasn't very musical, yet this is a mentality that many guitarists get trapped in. I always felt that the worst shred guitar solos were the ones where the guitarist mentally checked off the techniques on a list… "Here are my tapping ideas … here's my legato ideas … here's my picking bit…" The guitarists who spoke to me were the ones who didn't use solos to demonstrate their technique, but the ones who used their technique to make powerful music.

So, I began working on exercises that allowed me to combine the things I knew more seamlessly, and before I knew it, music became magical again.

Let me show you what I mean.

First, we need to make sure that we know both our arpeggio and our scale. Here they are for a Cmaj7 chord.

Example 8a:

Many people like to think of arpeggios as something you "take out" of a scale. I.e., the notes of a Cmaj7 arpeggio are found within the C Major scale:

(C) D (E) F (G) A (B) (C)

But I prefer to think of scales as the notes that *connect* my arpeggios. The arpeggio notes are the target notes, and the scale notes fill in the gaps between them. It's a subtle shift in perspective, but it's incredibly useful when it comes to thinking about note choice when we're soloing.

Let's explore this idea by playing parts of the arpeggio and filling in the gaps with scale tones.

Example 8b:

The secret exercise that will supercharge your visualisation here is to ascend four notes of the arpeggio, then descend four notes of the scale.

For example, we ascend the arpeggio notes:

1 3 5 7

Then descend the scale intervals:

6 5 4 3

Next, we return to the arpeggio and ascend again. Since we finished on the 3rd (an arpeggio tone), we don't want to repeat that note, so we jump to the 5th and ascend:

5 7 1 3

Then we descend the scale:

2 1 7 6

Here, I prefer to jump up to the root rather than the 7th because the 7th can sound weak. This causes us to repeat the whole patten an octave higher. The entire exercise looks like this:

Example 8c:

This exercise is fascinating because even though we're playing all seven notes of the major scale, it still feels like an arpeggio idea because four of the seven notes are chord tones, so the lines naturally outline the sound of the chord. This doesn't just train your fingers, it trains your ear as well.

Of course, we need to be able to do this across the neck. Here's the same idea played around the A and C shapes.

Example 8d:

The real magic of this exercise is how it subconsciously trains your ear. If we switch to a C7 chord and connect the arpeggio and scale with the same approach, we're suddenly playing the Mixolydian mode.

Let's do this but include a descending version this time. It's the same principle as before, but now we'll descend four notes of the arpeggio and ascend four notes of the scale in the second half of the exercise.

Notice all the B notes are now Bb.

Example 8e:

This exercise not only develops your fretboard fluency, it helps blur the line between arpeggios and scales in a natural, musical way, so you can combine them organically in your solos.

As an aside, if we add a chromatic tone before the ascending arpeggio and mix up the rhythm, we can instantly create some really cool-sounding vocabulary that works great over a blues chord sequence. I use these kinds of ideas as springboards for improvisation because they're perfect for establishing the tonality and setting a line in motion.

Example 8f:

Here's that C7 sound, but now outlined in both the A and C shapes.

Example 8g:

Mixolydian is the most commonly associated scale sound with a dominant 7 chord, but it's not the only one we can use. Another option is Phrygian Dominant. Instead of learning this as a new scale with new fingerings, we can simply adjust the descending scale notes to match the scale formula: 1 b2 3 4 5 b6 b7.

So, let's connect our arpeggio notes with a b2, 4, and b6 instead.

Here's that idea laid out on the fretboard around the E shape. Try to hear the intervals before you play them.

Example 8h:

This approach can be applied to any scale as long as we understand the intervals (which I assume you have a reasonable grip on if you're reading this book).

For example, there's nothing to say we *must* connect major 7 arpeggios with notes from the major scale. We could use the Lydian scale instead (like the major scale but with a #4). Listen to how the one small change of adding the #4 (F#) changes the sound of a Cmaj7 vamp.

Example 8i:

Cmaj7#11

```
T--------------------------------------------------7------------8-12-10-8-7-------
A----------4--------------------5-9-7-5-----------8---10-8-7-----8-12-----------10---
B------5------7-5-4------5-9----------------9-7--9-------------------------------
------3-7------------7----------------9-7--10--------------------------------------
```

Now we know we can connect arpeggios that spell out the chord using different notes, let's look at what we can do on a minor 7 chord.

Minor chords can be confusing at first because they work differently depending on their function in a key. For instance, sometimes they function as the ii chord in a key and sometimes as the vi.

The ii chord is a Dorian scale sound (1 2 b3 4 5 6 b7), and the vi chord is Aeolian (1 2 b3 4 5 b6 b7). The chord function affects which notes we use to connect our arpeggios.

As Dorian is slightly more common, we'll start there. Dorian has a natural 6th, so our connecting scale tones will be the 2, 4, and 6.

Example 8j:

Cm7

```
T-----------------------------------------8-11-10-8----------8-11-10-8----------
A-----------------------8-7-------------8----------10-8---8-11----------11-10---
B--------8-7------8-10---------10-8-7--10-------------------------------------
-----8-11-----10-8------10---------------------------------------------------
```

If we replace the natural 6th with a b6, we create the darker Aeolian sound. You already know where the b6 is from the Phrygian Dominant earlier in the routine, we're just using it in a minor chord now.

Example 8k:

Let's extend these ideas a bit. In this next exercise, we'll play through each of the diatonic chords in the key of C Major, using scale notes to connect them when descending. For example, we'll ascend Cmaj7, descend the scale, ascend Dm7, descend the scale, and so on.

This exercise is a perfect blend of scales and arpeggios and shows how they can coexist.

Example 8l:

Em7   **Fmaj7**   **G7**   **Cmaj7**

```
E|------7-10-8-7------------8-12-10-8-7--------------10-13-12-10----------------|
B|----8-----------10-8------------------10------8-12-----------13-12------13----|
G|--9-------------------------10-----------------------------------------------|
D|-----------------------------------------------------------------------------|
A|-----------------------------------------------------------------------------|
E|-----------------------------------------------------------------------------|
```

You can do this same idea in different positions, like around the A shape.

Example 8m:

Cmaj7   **Dm7**   **Em7**   **Fmaj7**

```
E|-------------------------------------------------3----------------5-3-----------|
B|----------4-2----------2-5-4-2----------4--5-4-2------------2-5---------5-4-2-----|
G|------2-5---------5-3-2--------3----2-5-----------5------3-----------------------|
D|--3--------------5-----------------------------------------------------------------|
A|-----------------------------------------------------------------------------------|
E|-----------------------------------------------------------------------------------|
```

G7   **Am7**   **Bm7♭5**   **Cmaj7**

```
E|----------------------------------3--------------------5-3-----------------|
B|------3-6-5-3------------5---6-5-3----------3-6----6-5-3--------------5------|
G|----4---------5-4----2-5---------------5-4---------------------------------|
D|--5-----------------------------------------------------------------------|
A|-----------------------------------------------------------------------------|
E|-----------------------------------------------------------------------------|
```

This idea also works horizontally across the neck, which can really test your fretboard knowledge.

As you do this, think about and visualise each chord in the key and connect them with notes from the C Major scale, rather than thinking about a different mode for each chord.

Example 8n:

To finish this week, let's take the chord sequence from *Fly Me to the Moon* and learn how we can combine our arpeggios and scales in a more fluid manner.

The first step is outlining the chord progression with only arpeggios. Here, I played through the progression in just one of the infinite ways possible. Copying this example will help you to learn, but figuring out your own approach will be the most valuable practice, so make sure to explore your own creative approaches.

Example 8o:

Now, if we add rhythmic variety to some arpeggio and scale combinations we can create a more melodic approach.

You could spend a lifetime refining your phrasing with this concept, and that's the journey most of us end up on in our playing, as we constantly practice these ideas over more tunes.

Normally, the melody of the tune we're playing guides the shape and rhythmic ideas in our solos. It's all about repeating this process until you can smoothly outline your chord changes in a convincing way that relates to the melody of the song.

Example 8p:

There are no shortcuts here, you just need to put in the time. Minutes turn into hours, hours into days, and days into weeks. But if you focus on getting a little better each day, mastery becomes inevitable.

Keep at it!

Routine Nine: Extended Arpeggios

As we discovered in the chord book in this series, one of the most interesting ways to create complex sounds in harmony is to look to extended chords. The same goes for arpeggios, where we have multiple options for incorporating richer sounds.

A very simple way of extending an arpeggio and adding colour is to take the triad and add just one more note. For example, we can add a 9th interval to a C major triad to turn it into a Cadd9 arpeggio, giving us the intervals:

1 3 5 9

Or, if we confine those intervals to a single octave:

1 2 3 5

This idea creates the simplest form of extended arpeggio, but they sound wonderful. These should be learned around our three basic positions so that we can play them comfortably in any key.

Example 9a:

The previous example showed the extended arpeggio in vertical form, but they also work well in horizontal form. In fact, they allow us to cover a little more range and sound a bit like the iconic *Final Fantasy* prelude arpeggios!

Learn these starting on both the E and A string.

Example 9b:

Cadd9

```
T                   8—10—12—10—8
                8                   8
            5—7—9               9—7———5
A        5                           5
B  3—5—7                       7—5—3
                               3—0—3        3
```

```
                        12—15—20—15
                   13—15            17—15———13
            10—12—14       12            12
T        10                       14—12—10
A  8—10—12                            10
B                               12—10      8
```

We can apply the same concept to minor triads by adding the 9th, resulting in the intervals:

1 2 b3 5

So, a C minor add9 arpeggio across three positions looks like this:

Example 9c:

Cmadd9

```
                        3———8        8—3
                   3—4             4—3
T            5                       5
A        5                       5
B  3—5—6                       6—5———3
```

```
                        8        8
                   7—8       8—7
T            10                  10
A        10                      10
B  8—10—11                   11—10      8
```

When played in horizontal patterns, they lay out on the fretboard like this.

Example 9d:

At this point, it's worth considering again: when does an arpeggio start to feel like a scale?

Even though these arpeggio patterns contain three consecutive scale tones, they still function as arpeggios in my view. For example, in a chord progression like A – F#m – D – E, you can outline each chord with an add9 arpeggio starting from the root. Over the course of the progression, you play all seven notes of the A Major scale, but you're breaking them up into arpeggios that correspond directly to the harmony.

Example 9e:

Here's a longer example outlining that same progression twice. This time, I've added a few notes outside of the basic add9 arpeggios to make it more melodic. Let's break down this idea:

- In bar one, I use the b3 as a passing tone to approach the 3rd, and a 4th to connect the 5th down to the 3rd

- In bar three, there's a bluesy b5 to 4 slide that transitions down the F#m triad

- Bar five features a descending scale, leading to the 3rd of the E major chord in the next bar

- In bar 7, I use a 4th–b3–3rd targeting idea, plus a 4th to connect the 5th and 3rd again

- Bar 11 introduces the b7 of F#m, leading into the root in bar twelve, which could be interpreted as part of an F#m9 arpeggio

- Finally, bar fourteen ends with either the b7 of E major or another 4th–b3–3rd figure leading into the 3rd of A major in the next bar, depending on how you choose to view it

What I want you to take from this is that we don't have to be rigid with arpeggios. We can add embellishment notes to make our lines more dynamic and interesting.

Example 9f:

Why am I calling these add9 arpeggios, rather than just major 9 and minor 9?

Think back to the chord book and you'll recall that we learned the names of chords based on the highest extension when the 7th is present.

A chord built from the intervals 1 3 5 9 is simply a triad with an added 9th (no 7th).

If we include the 7th, so that we have 1 3 5 7 9, that's a major 9 chord.

So, we can make the major 9 sound either by adding one note to a major triad, or by playing a five-note arpeggio. Here we're playing a Cmaj9 (C E G B D) five-note arpeggio:

Example 9g:

We can extend this to a ii–V–I progression by playing minor 9, dominant 9, and major 9 arpeggios for each chord type.

Example 9h:

If we look at five-note arpeggios more closely, we can also view them as slash chords. In other words, an arpeggio superimposed over a bass note. For example, a Cmaj9 arpeggio can be viewed as an Em7 arpeggio played over a C bass note, or Em7/C in chord terms.

(C) E G B D

How does this information help us? Well, it allows us to play something we already know well (an Em7 arpeggio) and use it to create a different sound.

The key is to understand where to place this arpeggio relative to the root. In this case, to create a major 9 sound, we play a minor 7th arpeggio starting from the 3rd of the major chord (for C, that's E).

To understand why this works, we have to shift our perspective of the intervals. In the case of an Em7 arpeggio (1 b3 5 b7), the context changes when played over a C root. Here, E no longer sounds like the root (1), because now it's the 3rd of C. Similarly, G is no longer the b3, it's the 5th of C, and so on.

This is such a common arpeggio that we give it a name – the 3-to-9 arpeggio – because we're arpeggiating from the 3rd to the 9th of the chord.

Let's apply this idea to the three most basic chord types.

For each one I'll play the 1, then I'll say, "3 5 7 9" on the recording and play those intervals in relation to the chord.

Over a major 7 chord it will be 3 5 7 9.

Over a dominant 7 chord it will be 3 5 b7 9.

Over a minor 7 chord it will be b3 5 b7 9.

Example 9i:

You may have noticed that I didn't include a minor 7b5 chord in that demonstration. Why? The minor 7b5 chord gives us more options to explore. In a major scale, the 9th on a minor 7b5 chord is actually a b9, which doesn't always sound pleasing. So, when playing a 3-to-9 arpeggio over a minor 7b5 chord, I often play it as b3 b5 b7 9, turning it into a minor 9b5 arpeggio.

These kinds of choices always exist. For example, over a dominant chord, we can play 3 5 b7 9, but if we want a darker sound, we can instead play 3 5 b7 b9 for a 7b9 arpeggio.

Example 9j:

Now, let's revisit the *Fly Me to the Moon* progression from earlier, but this time we'll ascend 3-to-9 arpeggios over each chord:

- For major 7 chords we'll play a minor 7 arpeggio from the 3rd

- For minor 7 chords we'll play a major 7 arpeggio from the b3

- For dominant chords we'll play a diminished 7th arpeggio from the 3rd (for a 7b9 sound)

- For minor 7b5 chords we'll play a minor 7 arpeggio from the b3

Example 9k:

Dm9   **G7♭9**   **Cmaj9**

Bm7♭5(♭9)   **E7♭9**   **Am9**   **E7♭9**

Exercises like this are great because they force our brain to work out what we have to play, while we're playing it.

In the last example, we played the 3-to-9 arpeggios in ascending order, but keep in mind, as long as you're using the 3rd, 5th, 7th and 9th, it's still considered a 3-to-9 arpeggio, no matter the note order.

One way I like to break up this pattern is with octave displacement. Instead of playing the 3rd then ascending through 5, 7 and 9, I'll play the 3rd, followed by the 5th an octave lower, then ascend 5 7 9.

This time I'll play two beats of a chord tone, then play our 3-to-9 arpeggios with octave displacement.

Example 9l:

Am7   **Dm7**   **G7**   **Cmaj7**

Fmaj7   **Bm7♭5**   **E7**   **Am7**

This approach opens up new melodic possibilities and helps us to break free from repetitive patterns.

Now that we've discussed 9th arpeggios, it's time to explore 11th and 13th arpeggios. These extended arpeggios allow us to further enrich our sound, and while there are various ways to approach them methodically, I want to introduce what I call my "ultimate arpeggio patterns".

Our harmonic system is based on stacking 3rd intervals, called *tertian harmony*. If we build a 7th chord and continue stacking up the 3rds, we get:

1 3 5 7 9 11 13

This sequence covers all seven notes of the scale.

But if we're playing all the notes of the scale, how is this different from simply playing the scale itself? The distinction lies in thinking vertically – structuring these notes as stacked intervals rather than running them sequentially, as we would for a scale.

Let's take the C Mixolydian scale as an example. Here are the notes of the scale:

C D E F G A Bb

If we stack the notes in 3rds we get:

C E G Bb D F A

That forms a C13 arpeggio.

To me, this is the best way to internalise any scale, because it allows us to hear the harmony as a *vertical structure*.

When you think "C Mixolydian", I want you to hear the sound of C13. That's what this mode represents sonically – a rich, extended C dominant sound.

Let's apply this to the fretboard now.

Example 9m:

The key is to focus on the concept of stacking 3rds. No matter where you are on the neck, if you're playing over a C7 chord, you can stack thirds from the C Mixolydian mode to create that lush C13 sound.

In the next example, I'm using all seven notes of the scale, but the line emphasises stacked 3rds and we're playing through fingering fragments you've worked on in this book.

Example 9n:

The best way to practice this concept is to pick a key – let's stay in C to keep things simple –and, starting on each note of the C Major scale (C D E F G A B), stack notes in 3rds as you move up the neck.

This exercise has a double payoff. First, it helps you develop the ability to think vertically and create these extended arpeggios. Second, it trains your fingers to navigate these patterns efficiently. Remember, a concept is only as useful as your ability to execute it quickly, without hesitation.

Example 9o:

There's a lot to unpack here, and we're still just scratching the surface, but I don't want to go too much deeper. It makes more sense to master the core concepts you'll use regularly in your playing. However, you can take away these ideas and work on them whenever you want to explore further.

Take your time working on stacking 3rds and incorporating different extensions into your playing. When we return for the final week, we'll be working on etudes that will pull together all the concepts in the previous routines, so you better be ready!

Routine Ten: Putting It All Together Etudes

So, you've made it to the final week! Here's where we bring everything together and apply what we've learned with a collection of etudes over different chord progressions.

Any time you run into a problem with this routine, don't be afraid to go back to the where the concept was first introduced and refresh your memory. Remember, mastery of this subject is all about *knowing* the stuff. You won't have nailed this routine until you instinctively understand and *know* the concepts in it. If that means going back because you found a weak spot, excellent! That's just you working to eliminate your weaknesses.

We'll start this routine with the simplest of progressions, based on a classic pop-rock progression you might hear in a song like *Sweet Child O' Mine* or *Sweet Home Alabama*.

We're going to outline the following chords:

D major – C major – G major – D major

Our first etude will stick just to the notes of the triads, but we'll cover a lot of the neck doing it. Limitations like this really put our knowledge to the test.

Example 10a:

Some people say triads are boring, but that's not fair. It's not even right to call them simple – they are harmonically strong and the purest sound of a chord. Sure, you might want to add more complexity, and that's fine, but triads give you a solid foundation to build on.

We could, for example, treat each of those major chords as add9 chords and mix in our 1 2 3 5 arpeggio ideas.

Example 10b:

To make these etudes more musical, we can break up the rhythm a little. Long runs of 1/8th notes can get monotonous. I'll also introduce chromatic approach notes, often targeting the 3rd by approaching it with a b3 a semitone below.

Example 10c:

In the last etude for this progression, we'll throw theory out the window and treat all three chords as dominant chords. Technically, there should only be one dominant chord in a key, so how can we play three different dominant chord sounds here? The easy answer is that making everything dominant is a very blues or gospel thing to do – it's a familiar sound, even if it's not strictly "correct".

Example 10d:

Now let's move on to a different chord progression. This time it's a slightly jazzier take on a 12-bar blues. I've added a move to the VI chord in bar eight and replaced the V–IV move in bars 9-10 with a ii–V progression. This allows us to target a few more chords with our arpeggios.

We'll start by outlining the progression with arpeggios from the root note.

Example 10e:

If we decide to start every new chord from the 3rd, we can work on applying our 3-to-9 arpeggios. These can be played as straight ascending ideas, or with octave displacement.

Outside of those obvious 3-to-9s, I've also included some chromatic passing tones and scalar ideas because arpeggios should never exist in a vacuum – we're always looking to combine things to make them musical.

Example 10f:

D7 · A7 · F#7b9

Bm7 · E7b9 · A7 · E7b9 · A7

Our next etude expands on this 3-to-9 idea by alternating between 1-to-7 and 3-to-9 arpeggios over each chord. The big difference is we're going to focus on outlining the 7b9 chords by using diminished 7 arpeggios when they happen. So, you're getting to work on two things now.

Example 10g:

A7 · D7 · A7

D7 · A7 · F#7b9

Bm7 · E7b9 · A7 · E7b9 · A7

Now I'm going to blend our arpeggios and scalar ideas in a bit more depth.

We're using 3-to-9 arpeggios in the first two bars, then something a little closer to a straight A7 in bar three.

In bar four, I use a diminished 7 arpeggio to make the A7 an A7b9.

Bars five and six both use 3-to-9 arpeggios, both with octave displacement, and straight arpeggios.

Over the A7 in bar seven, we're playing a C#m7b5 in descending groups of four, which we transition into a Gdim7 in fours over the F#7b9.

Example 10h:

To finish up looking at arpeggios on the blues progression, I want to limit us to the "ascending arpeggio descending scale" concept we looked at in Routine 8. We don't always have to ascend up from the 1 either. If you look in the first measure, we ascend up a 3-to-9 arpeggio then come down the Mixolydian scale. We want to be able to do this with arpeggios starting on any note in the chord.

Example 10i:

Now I'd like to move on to the first sixteen bars of the progression for *Back Home Again in Indiana*. This is a great little progression that includes three of our important chord qualities, and has both functioning and non-functioning dominant chords. Your first step should be to memorise the chord progression, both as named chords and how it sounds. The best way to do this is always with just straight ascending arpeggios, so we'll start there.

Example 10j:

When you have this down, it makes sense to shift up to 3-to-9 arpeggios. When doing this, I'll treat the Eb7 and F7 as 7b9 chords, because they're resolving dominant chords, so we're using diminished 7 arpeggios on those. This is a great way to delve a little further into a chord progression before developing your lines over it in more detail.

Example 10k:

That might have felt like a lot of brain work, right? But we can dial back the mental stress by breaking up our rhythms and leaving a little more space.

Here, I'll start with a 3-to-9 over the Abmaj7 with 1/4 notes, then a straight F7b9 arpeggio over the F7, and an arpeggio-scale combination over the Bb7.

Over the Bbm7, I play a 3-to-9 idea with both octave and rhythmic displacement. This leads us to the Eb7 chord, and over this, I'm actually playing the #5, 3, #9 and b9 – that's a lot of tension! Drawing altered chord ideas from the Super Locrian mode always gives us options. Bar nine outlines the Dbmaj7 chord with a Db major triad, and I add chromatic approach notes, which happen to also be in the key.

Example 10l:

Now let's look at one of the more popular melodies played over these changes. I'm particularly fond of bars five through eight. If you look closely, you'll see a Bbm9 arpeggio, the 3-to-9 Bbm7 with octave displacement, an Eb+ triad, a Cm7, and an Ebm9 arpeggio. That's a lot of cool arpeggios woven together!

Example 10m:

For our last couple of examples, I want to up the challenge by focusing on something where we need to play two chords per bar. There are lots of examples of that, but we're going to look at John Coltrane's iconic *Giant Steps*.

This is a tune that has a reputation for being one of the big bogeyman of jazz, but I like to think about Joe Pass's take on it. He said people sometimes ask for *Giant Steps*, but they don't really know what they're asking for – it's just a challenge. He didn't like to work too hard, so he'd play it as a bossa!

As with all the previous examples, the best place to start is by playing ascending arpeggios. This is going to be much harder now because there's no breathing room between chords.

Example 10n:

Now let's up the ante by ascending one arpeggio then connecting it to the nearest note in the next arpeggio and descending. We're not worried about playing in root position here, we're just focusing on connecting one arpeggio to the next. It's a real visualisation nightmare!

Example 10o:

Ebmaj7   Am7   D7   Gmaj7   C#m7   F#7

Bmaj7   Fm7   Bb7   Ebmaj7   C#m7   F#7

There are obviously limitless ways to outline these changes. I like to think of it like a gigantic plinko board: you drop your token in at the top, and you never quite know which path it's going to take to the bottom. That's the exciting part: knowing that anything can happen.

Example 10p:

Bmaj7   D7   Gmaj7   Bb7   Ebmaj7   Am7   D7

Gmaj7   Bb7   Ebmaj7   F#7   Bmaj7   Fm7   Bb7

In that example, I tried to be even less tied down. There are some chromatic connections and scalar ideas, plus a cool drop 2 voiced arpeggio to start. I might use that as a springboard to arpeggiate through the whole progression with drop 2 voicings, or play 3-to-9s on every chord, or focus on approaching all the chords chromatically.

Whatever takes my fancy, as part of my own practice sessions I will sit down with pen and paper and write out a new etude, then work on that idea. I'll learn it, then I'll throw the paper away and forget it. For the next session, I'll write something new. That's because it's always about working on the skill of creating, never just remembering something composed. If we keep pushing like that, our brains will never stop improving.

And there we have it, the end of 10 weeks! But it's not over… it's never over!

Conclusion

It's been a long road, but you've finally made it! If you've been working through this for ten weeks or more, give yourself a pat on the back, you've certainly earned it.

Now, with that out of the way, let's get real. Real-life music isn't like a book with a neat, tidy ending. Music is an ever-evolving art form, a way to express ourselves, and it's an unending task – the learning never stops. But here's the thing: you've now got the tools to continue forward and be your own guide in your studies.

You can now pull up the chord progression to any song and dig into it; play the chords, mess around with the arpeggios, explore the scales. You can think about how the chords work together and what options they offer you as a player.

Remember, music is a language, and the best way to learn it is to listen to how it's spoken, to speak it yourself, and ideally to speak it with others. Study the greats. Whether it's Jason Becker or Pat Martino, it doesn't matter. Listen to how your favourite players use these words to speak and you'll hear scales, chords, and arpeggios being used in all different ways. The more you listen, the more your ears will get trained, and soon enough you'll be able to hear something on a record or in your head, and instantly connect it to your guitar. You'll hear an idea and *bam*, you'll be able to play it.

It all comes down to knowing your intervals inside-out and having a solid relationship with your instrument, so that applying those intervals becomes second nature. Yes, that takes time! But you've already put in months of work, training this stuff subconsciously, so trust me, you've got what it takes.

If there's one thing I believe after twenty years of playing, teaching countless students, and rubbing shoulders with some of the best players in the world, is that there's no such thing as talent. The only people who talk about talent are the ones looking for excuses to explain why they can't do something.

The truth is, it all comes down to hard work, passion and repetition. Keep working at it, day after day. Every time you pick up the guitar, just aim to be a little bit better than you were yesterday. With that approach, success isn't just a possibility, it's guaranteed.

Get out there, keep playing, and good luck!

Levi

www.ingramcontent.com/pod-product-compliance
Lightning Source LLC
Chambersburg PA
CBHW081429090426

42740CB00017B/3244